I0493357

CEO Guide to Doing Business in India

By Ade Asefeso MCIPS MBA

Copyright 2014 by Ade Asefeso MCIPS MBA
All rights reserved.

Second Edition

ISBN-13: 978-1499542974

ISBN-10: 1499542976

Publisher: AA Global Sourcing Ltd
Website: http://www.aaglobalsourcing.com

Table of Contents

Disclaimer

This publication is designed to provide competent and reliable information regarding the subject matter covered. However, it is sold with the understanding that the author and publisher are not engaged in rendering professional advice. The authors and publishers specifically disclaim any liability that is incurred from the use or application of contents of this book.

If you purchased this book without a cover you should be aware that this book may have been stolen property and reported as "unsold and destroyed" to the publisher. In this case neither the author nor the publisher has received any payment for this "stripped book."

Dedication

This book is dedicated to the hundreds of thousands of incredible souls in the Western world who have weathered through the up and down of seeing their jobs moved to India.

To Maureen Asefeso who seem to have been sent here to teach me something about who I am supposed to be. She have nurtured me, challenged me, and even opposed me.... But at every juncture has taught me!

This book is dedicated to my lovely boys, Thomas, Michael and Karl. Teaching them to manage their finance will give them the lives they deserve. They have taught me more about life, presence, and energy management than anything I have done in my life.

Chapter 1: Why India?

Are you a CEO, consultant, or entrepreneur interested in entering or expanding your business activity in India?

Interested in entering or expanding your activity in the India market; then this book is for you.

The main objective of this book is to provide you with basic knowledge about India; an overview of its economy, business culture, potential opportunities and an introduction to other relevant issues. Novice exporters, in particular will find it a useful starting point.

Some countries may be subject to export restrictions due to sanctions and embargoes placed on them by the UN or EU. Exporting companies are responsible for checking that their goods can be exported and that they are using the correct licences.

While Mumbai and New Delhi continue to be the biggest contributing hubs to India's economy, emerging cities outperform the metros in terms of GDP growth. The Tier II cities hold the key to India's future growth and offer many profitable opportunities to foreign businesses.

Indian Companies in India's emerging cities are quickly developing an appetite for know-how, infrastructure, and venture capital, seeking to capture the benefits of India's economic development. Many

Indian companies are open to the prospects of international partnerships and are often highly diversified.

India's growth story is getting better known. 20 years ago, it was China and the Far East that dominated the growth story.

India's growth has accelerated as the Indian domestic market has expanded rapidly and Indian companies are venturing overseas...

Indian companies now find it easier to raise finance in the UK because of three main factors:
- Time advantage
- Legal advantage and
- Language advantage

As we have seen in recent years UK economy has stepped away from traditional manufacturing and shifted towards more value-added, specialised industries, a trend forecast to continue, hence more and more India companies are raising finance in the UK.

UK is a leading provider of financial and business services, sectors that contribute significantly to the local and national economies of India, both in terms of output and employment.
Below are four of UK's key sectors identified as offering a competitive edge in India:

Education and skills

Higher education, vocational skills, accreditation and qualifications providers, teaching aids and technologies.

Retail and supply chain logistics

Single brand apparel, food and beverage, supply chain solutions and technologies, back end systems.

Financial and professional business services

Financial, accounting and legal services, PR, management consulting.

Creative and Media

Film, gaming and animation, design, digital advertising and mobile content development, e-content, and marketing.

I will elaborate more on all of the above 4 key sectors later in this book!

UK businesses have paid some attention to India's emerging cities but traditionally it has been within the cities' core sectors, for instance ICT in Bangalore or mining in Kolkata. However, as emerging cities grow and diversify their industries, they offer new and exciting opportunities across a variety of sectors. In this book, the cities of Hyderabad, Pune, Bangalore, Chennai, and Kolkata are presented as ideal destinations for pioneering in emerging sectors.

These cities have been selected due to their growing potential and because they offer good infrastructure and visibility.

Chapter 2: Strengths of the Market

In India's emerging cities, I encouraged UK businesses to seize the cities' advantages such as their low costs and low competitive environment.

The figures for UK FDI with India at end-2009 (stock) are:

- UK stock of investment in India £9,310 million;
- Indian stock of investment in UK £1,841 million.

[Source: ONS MA4]

UK Exports to India (source: HMRC)

Year	£million
2006	2,704
2007	2,964
2008	4,119
2009	2,893
2010	3,547

UK Imports from India (source: HMRC)

Year	£million
2006	3,188
2007	3,773
2008	4,266
2009	4,325
2010	5,032

Chapter 3: Opportunities in India

India may be a complex and challenging market but it is one that cannot be ignored by UK companies that are seeking to expand and go international.

India is the second fastest growing economy, after China. The business opportunities, which a few years ago, existed only in the traditional economic heartlands of Mumbai, Delhi and Bangalore have now stretched to the emerging cities of Nagpur, Ahmedabad, Chandigarh, Pune and Jaipur, to name but a few.

There are opportunities in the next generation cities in India where UK companies can build long term relationships in the coming times. The World Bank predicted that India will be the fastest growing economy in 2011 at about 8%.

India is full of opportunities, some very visible and some still to be unearthed. As long as we are able to find innovative solutions and creative collaborations, the trade and investment relation between India and the UK will keep growing.

Huge investment potential exists in various sectors such as life sciences, manufacturing, energy, and infrastructure among others. Ernst and Young recognises India as one of the emerging biotech leaders, ranked third in the Asia-Pacific region based on the number of biotech companies in the country.

The Biotech Industry in India has a growth rate of 37% per annum; one of the highest in the world. The market size of Indian Pharma Industry is estimated to reach £14.39 billion by 2011. The Indian Infrastructure sector has the potential to absorb US $500 billion in FDI by 2012.

The Indian telecom industry is growing at the fastest pace in the world and India is expected to become the second largest telecom market by 2012. Over 10 million mobile handsets sold per month. India has emerged as the 2nd largest market after China for mobile-phone handsets.

Automobile industry in India is one of the fastest growing automobile industries and is predicted to be among the top five vehicle producers by 2014. From the unveiling of the world's lowest-cost car, the Nano, in January 2009 to the acquisition of the Jaguar and Land Rover brands in March 2009.

India's presence on the global automotive market cannot be questioned. The industry has witnessed an influx of both global equipment manufacturers as well as Tier 1 component manufacturers, who are setting up their manufacturing bases in the country. The Indian auto components industry has also grown by more than five-fold over the last decade.

Chapter 4: Seizing the Opportunities

As with any new market, going into India requires due diligence and research on customers, market channels, promotion and advertising, product demand, etc.

Local knowledge is paramount.

A good network of contacts is essential to doing business in India. Taking part in events and trade delegations is a good strategy and has proven to be a stepping stone to success for many businesses.

Challenges of doing business in emerging cities of India

While India's emerging cities offer many opportunities, they may also pose certain challenges.

These challenges can be managed and should not deter you from taking your business beyond the Indian metros.

Infrastructure

This remains one of the key issues affecting companies in emerging cities; power interruptions, roads in poor condition and scarcity of international flight connections being the top three challenges.

The government is allocating huge amounts of investment towards road construction and green field airports.

State incentives can include uninterrupted electricity supply to attract foreign investment.
Emerging cities also have the advantage of newer infrastructure with fresh investment going towards building modern roads and buildings.

Depending on each business' format, tier-II cities could be much more advantageous than metros if located near ports, industrial corridors or important R&D hubs.

Workforce

Emerging cities offer a smaller talent pool compared to the metros, but cost of labour is considerably lower. In addition, while metros may seem to offer a large and attractive talent pool, professionals are more ambitious, more money-driven and there is much competition amongst employers to capture the best available talent. Staff turnover is also much lower in emerging cities where people appreciate a good employer closer to home, providing the stability that your business requires.

Business networks

Businesses in emerging cities are thriving, but networks still exist at the very early stages. Getting to know the right contacts and partners can take some time. Fortunately, smaller cities grant your business more visibility, and ease of travel (low traffic) allows you to have more frequent meetings.

Foreign players in emerging cities have tapped into this first-player advantage by setting up business networks, for example the British Business Groups, hence increasing their contact base and influence.

In terms of market entry barriers, India's regulatory framework is standardised and enforced across India. Such is the case for FDI regulations and legal business structures. India's legal system is very similar to UK's legal system.

Chapter 5: Economic Overview

India opened up the economy in the early nineties following a major crisis that was led by a foreign exchange crunch that dragged the economy close to defaulting on loans.

The response was a slew of domestic and external sector policy measures partly prompted by the immediate needs and partly by the demand of the multilateral organisations. The Indian economy responded well to these measures as annual GDP growth started averaging over 6% in the 1990s, well above the 'Hindu growth rate' of 3% in the previous four decades.

This moved upwards to an 8.5%+ growth trajectory in the 2002-03 to the 2007-08 period with the GDP shares of agriculture, manufacturing and services constituting 18%, 29% and 53% respectively.

The high growth rates also saw India's per capita incomes growing by over 4% per annum, making India the world's twelfth largest economy by market exchange rates and the fourth largest in PPP terms (2003) after US, China & Japan.

Liberalisation also triggered the growth of a rapidly expanding consumer class. The increased use of consumer durables portrays this feature appropriately. The global financial crisis squarely hit the Indian economy as it slowed down to 6.7% in 2008-09. Currently i.e. in 2009-10 the economy clawed back and is set to achieve a 7.2% growth. Indian

Government now eyes an 8.5% growth in 2010-11 and a return to 9%+ growth in 2011-12 onwards.

Trade and investment are increasingly becoming important components of the economy as GDP growth sets to reach new highs of double digit growth. While managing high rates of overall growth there is a growing perception that growth continues to be unevenly distributed. Some states like Karnataka, Andhra Pradesh, Tamil Nadu, Gujarat and Maharashtra continue to grow at a faster rate than their populous counterparts such as Bihar, Madhya Pradesh and Uttar Pradesh.

Unemployment and income disparities continue to trap around 25% of the population below the poverty line.

Economic Policy changes

The new policy regime since 1991 radically pushed forward in favour of a more open and market oriented economy.

India has removed most of her trade barriers. The peak tariff rate is down to 10% in 2009-10 from 72% in 1991, while quantitative restrictions on imports ended in 2001, opening up the economy to foreign businesses, especially in consumer goods. This also meant more foreign capital flowing into India.

The cumulative FDI flows into India from April 2000 to December 2009 stands at about US $110 billion. Indeed India's slow paced yet consistent reform programme has increased external and internal competition.

The public sector role both as producer and consumer of goods and services although still significant is declining. It still accounts for a quarter of GDP, one-third of investments and one-sixth of final consumption expenditure. This is expected to fall gradually as privatization and disinvestment programmes gain momentum in the coming years.

India's privatisation initiatives have enhanced the attractiveness of state-owned assets in sectors with a promising future such as telecoms, oil and gas, pharmaceuticals, real estate development and travel and tourism.

India's population is 1.2 billion approximately.

Chapter 6: Political Overview

The Indian Constitution provides a system of parliamentary and cabinet government both at the centre and in the states. The Indian Parliament consists of the President, as the constitutional head of the executive) and 2 Houses.

The Lower House - Lok Sabha ('House of the People') directly elected on the basis of universal adult suffrage; and the Upper House Rajya Sabha ('Council of States') indirectly elected by the members of state legislative assemblies.

The Bharatiya Janata Party (BJP) and the Congress Party are the 2 main forces in the current Indian political scene. Congress heads the ruling coalition at the centre, the United Progressive Alliance (UPA) while the BJP leads the Opposition alliance the National Democratic Alliance (NDA). Whilst neither can command a clear Parliamentary majority, following the UPA's good performance at the recent election, UPA gathered the extra seats to form the current government and enjoy a comfortable majority.

AA Global Sourcing Ltd http://www.aaglobalsourcing.com can provide:

- Export healths check to assess a company's readiness for exporting and help develop a plan of action.
- Training in the requirements for trading overseas.

- Access to an experienced local International Trade Adviser.
- Specialist help with tackling cultural and language issues when communicating with Indian customers and partners.
- Advice on how to go about market research and the possibility of a grant towards approved market-research projects.
- Ongoing support to help business continue to develop overseas trade and look at dealing with more sophisticated activities or markets.

AA Global Sourcing Ltd http://www.aaglobalsourcing.com services include the provision of market information, validated lists of agents/potential partners, key market players or potential customers; establishing the interest of such contacts in working with the company; and arranging appointments. In addition, they can also organise events for you to meet contacts or promote a company and its products/services.

Chapter 7: Priority Sectors and Indian Market Regulations

In the earlier chapter of this book I identified four key sectors based on output and contribution to UK's Gross Value Added (GVA).

UK businesses in these four sectors can offer a competitive advantage and export a wide array of products, services and expertise currently in high demand in India:

- Education and Skills
- Retail and Supply Chain Logistics
- Financial and Professional Business Services
- Creative and Media

Rising income levels and the changes in consumer choices are creating a greater demand for white goods, cars, mobile phones, leisure items, travel, shopping malls and Western brands. India matters with millions of affluent people and a growing middle-class presenting significant opportunities for UK businesses.

Thriving Indian businesses also present a great area of opportunity with many of them seeking for foreign services and expertise that can enable their expansion plans both within India and overseas.

Education is one of India's greatest challenges to date. The country has a population of 572 million people aged under 25 years of age (2008), of whom only 219 million children (37%) are enrolled in schools and 11 million attend colleges, a clear indication of the country's inability to meet demand. This gap in education provision and a great industry demand for a skilled workforce mean growing opportunities for education providers across areas.

The private sector has already stepped in to address the market gap, with businesses setting up sector-specific training institutes.

Ambitiously, India's Prime Minster has set a target to up skill 500 million Indians by 2022. India's economic expansion has developed existing industries and created new sectors which have in turn generated new employment opportunities and a subsequent demand for quality education.

The country's demographic composition and growing economy point to further growth in education and skills, a sector estimated to reach US$50 billion by 2015.

Now here are these opportunities made more evident than in emerging cities. Previously, education institutions in tier-II and III cities had very limited access to collaborative work with international partners or to provide international accreditations. However, the demand and talent are there, and students in these cities will favour degrees offered closer to home rather than enduring the costs of moving to a metro or overseas. Pune and Hyderabad are already profiling as two hubs for education in the subcontinent.

Chapter 8: Education and Skills

FDI in the education sector is 100% permitted.

The challenge for foreign investors is in the sector's regulatory framework. The forthcoming Foreign Education Providers Bill will liberalise the HR sector by allowing overseas universities to set up campuses in India but at present, accreditation for formal education providers is given only for 'not for-profit' organisations. As such, institutions must set up an entity that is legally permitted to generate profits or distribute profits via the education institution.

By contrast, non formal education providers such as coaching institutions, pre-schools, research institutes and vocational training are allowed to operate for-profit and are not regulated by a government body.

Higher education institutes must be affiliated to a local university and secure the proper accreditations by the Ministry of Human Resources Development (MHTD) and other relevant federal, state or discipline-specific bodies.

Market Regulations Opportunities

Higher Education: India presents opportunities in this segment for collaboration with Indian institutes, whether for joint delivery of courses, curriculum development, or student/staff exchanges. There is also a growing demand for validation of Indian qualifications. Foreign providers can find many business opportunities in knowledge sharing, consultancy and research.

Vocational Education and Skills Training

The vocational segment has emerged as a US$2.65 billion market and is expected to grow rapidly at an estimate of 25% per year. This is a thriving segment, and one that is required to quickly address the needs of the Indian population and increase their employability.

UK based institutions and those with strengths in niche areas such as accountancy, arts, law and healthcare would be well placed to venture into India's emerging cities.

Accreditation and Qualifications

Across areas, there is a growing demand for industry accreditation providers. There is great interest in accreditations in many sectors including healthcare, management, construction and accountancy.

Partnerships with the Private Sector

In order to meet education demands, many private companies have stepped in to address the education gap and to provide much needed quality training.

Public private partnership (PPP) frameworks have been well received and industry heavyweights across several sectors have set up schools and training institutes. In India, virtually every business is interested in education regardless of sector, and opportunities exist for curriculum development, consultancy, staff training and accreditations.

Teaching Aids and Technologies

With the emergence of private education providers, many grade and middle schools are competing on the basis of quality and technology. There is a growing demand for teaching aids such as e-content, multimedia, e-learning platforms and information and communications technology. The country's vast territory and largely rural population also underline the great need for technologies that support distance learning and e-learning.

A thriving economy has allowed Indian businesses to grow and explore new opportunities for expansion in India and overseas. This presents many opportunities for consultants, trainers and business services providers.

Indian businesses, particularly those in emerging cities, were previously unaware of or had limited access to partnerships with foreign providers. However, their emergence onto the global scene presents a vast and growing market. In India, virtually every business and sector is interested in education and training.

Opportunities exist for curriculum development, consultancy, staff training and accreditations. UK offers a wide range of consultants, professional training bodies, universities and institutions that can help the Indian workforce and businesses fill the existing skills gap.

Chapter 9: Retail and Supply Chain Logistics

Retail is a sector that sits close to our daily lives and affects us all. India is no exception. Most of us have heard of India's growth story.

It is a massive market growing at impressive rates. But what does this mean for UK retail businesses and in what areas can it succeed?

In a country with a middle class of 300 million people, growing disposable incomes and an appetite for foreign goods, the question should not be "are there opportunities for business?" but rather "where are they"? and "how do we harness them"?

The Indian retail sector is valued at £227 billion and is forecast to reach £352 billion by 2014 but looking past the numbers, the opportunities are perhaps being driven more strongly by the country's evolving consumer base.

India's new generation aspires to a more international lifestyle and they are keener to experience western-style shopping. This is perhaps more evident in India's metros, but emerging cities are catching up quickly.

The leading Indian cities in retail growth are: Pune, Hyderabad, Ludhiana, Bangalore and Chandigarh.

In terms of challenges, the Indian market remains complex. Most Indian outlets are independent, small-scale mum & dad or kirana stores. Roughly 95% of the retail sector is unorganised, and the rest is dominated by India's large retail players.

In India, there remain issues with poor infrastructure, logistics and transport; more than a third of total farm output is lost before it reaches the consumer.

FDI regulation and limits are applied on a format basis for single or multi-brand outlets and wholesale cash-and-carry operations. With retail being the second largest employer in the country and a general interest to develop the organized retail sector, further liberalisation of FDI can be expected.

- Wholesale: For over four years now, the Indian government has allowed 100% FDI in this segment. Retailers already in the market include: Wal-Mart's agreement with Bharti, and Tesco with Trent (Tata Group) for wholesale cash-and-carry operations which sell in bulk to other, smaller retailers.
- Single-brand retail: FDI is permitted up to the current FDI cap of 51% and with prior government approval. Overseas companies must therefore have a local partner. Marks & Spencer is already in the market and active in emerging cities. Other single-brand retailers operating under this scheme include Next, Mothercare and The Body Shop.

Multi-brand retail: For retail, this is where the FDI debate is taking place. At the moment FDI is not permitted for multi brand retailers and the only way into the country is with a local partner, setting up a franchise. Retail chain Debenhams has already adopted this approach. There are mixed views on when and how to liberalise this segment and the implications it would have on the local economy however, the general feeling is that everyone stands to gain from a more organised retail sector.

A common denominator of the opportunities in retail has to do with demand for consulting, training, management systems and technologies to improve distribution channels and supply chain.

There is room for knowledge transfer and for products and services that can increase efficiencies in India's supply chain. UK-based expertise is quite significant in this area, with more than 200 thousand employees in the logistics sector alone.

Back End Retail

With retail space forecast to double in the next few years, companies in the business of retail services can find an array of opportunities in India.

Figures by the Centre for Monitoring Indian Economy (CMIE) show that the average Indian household spends just over 25% of its income on food, but millions in the country remain spending more than half. The food and beverage segment therefore presents enormous potential.

Economic development has brought a faster paced lifestyle for young Indians who now demand more convenience foods thus creating yet more new areas of opportunity in food processing and distribution.

Opportunities

- Supply chain solutions and technologies.
- Management techniques and training for the retail supply chain.
- Consulting services to improve efficiencies.
- Shopping mall: engineering; shop fitting and design.
- CCTV entry systems; cash registers; stock control, racking and bar-coding systems.
- Food processing and packaging technology.
- Cold storage.
- Warehousing and distribution.

Front End Retail

Changing lifestyles and income growth have generated demand for international and luxury brands. Apparel and fashion are fast-growing segments as is demonstrated by the recent boom in retail space and a growing presence of foreign brands in the country.

Organised retail is estimated to be growing at over 20% annually and a large portion of India's new mall developments are expected to take place in India's emerging cities.

In terms of food outlets, there are currently over 200 food chains operating in India, with some of the foreign players counting: Costa Coffee, Subway, McDonald's and KFC. More than 50% of India's imported food and drink is at the moment consumed in the country's four largest metros, highlighting the latent opportunities in Tier-II cities.

Chapter 10: Financial and Professional Business Services

The Financial and Professional Business Services sector is one of the pillars of UK economy. With a declining participation of manufacturing industries in the UK GVA, the economy has shifted towards more value-added, knowledge based sectors. Nowadays, UK is a strong provider and trader of specialised services, particularly financial and business services.

Professional Services

While UK leads the world in professional services, India has become one of the world's biggest markets for professionals in this area. Economic progress, demography and an appetite for international business are all driving India's need for overseas know-how.

The rise of India's emerging cities and their economic diversification present opportunities for UK businesses in service delivery, partnerships and client-referral schemes across accountancy, legal, PR and management consulting.

Accountancy

The opportunity in accountancy is two-fold:
- Training and service provision. Given the high economic growth, Indian businesses and managers will increasingly need training on

international accountancy practices and standards.

- Opportunities also exist in the form of partnerships for client referrals or joint delivery of services such as tax advisory and compliance, corporate finance, forensic accounting, business recovery services, audit and assurance, asset management, and support for mergers and acquisitions.

Legal

Foreign lawyers are not permitted to practise in India. Currently, the sole recognised legal practitioner in the country is the advocate; a profession regulated by the Bar Council of India. Nonetheless, foreign lawyers are able to secure visas to visit clients and partners in the country, which is most beneficial to practitioners sustaining best-friend arrangements.

Entry barriers for lawyers are expected to relax once the Limited Liability Partnership Act comes into effect, whereby Indian and foreign law firms could form an LLP in India without limits on partners.

In India, there are opportunities for service provision to large players and Indian multinationals which are largely based in the Indian hubs, including Chennai, Kolkata, Hyderabad and Bangalore. UK law firms are well placed to offer services through client-referral or joint delivery schemes in Tier I and II cities in areas such as:

- International trade services
- International law

- Dispute resolution and arbitration
- Business litigation
- IP
- Labour law and
- Specialised legal services.

Public Relations

As Indian companies go global and international businesses invest in India, there will be an increased need for professional services in financial PR, publicity, industrial networking, etc. All of which are in scarce supply at the moment.

Indian Investment in the UK

More and more Indian businesses are establishing a presence in Europe. Long lasting ties between India and the UK, along with a relative ease to raise finance, make UK a top destination. Such was the case of India-based EXIM bank which recently relocated their European offices from Milan to London due to an unparalleled availability of talent, infrastructure and visibility on the global financial stage. Many such companies require the help of UK lawyers, bankers and accountants to set up their businesses and meet local regulations.

Banking and financial services

Financial services is one of the fastest growing sectors in the Indian economy. Most of the global players in Banking and Financial services are present in India e.g. Goldman Sachs, Morgan Stanley, Merrill Lynch,

JP Morgan, Deutsche Bank, UBS, Lehman Brothers, HSBC, Standard Chartered, Barclays, and Calyon.

The Reserve Bank of India (RBI) is the country's regulator for the Banking and Financial sector.

India has about 166 commercial banks (including 86 regional rural banks) and a network of 80,000 offices nationwide. Of these, about 40% are rural branches. State-owned banks account for approximately three quarters of total banking assets.

By assets, the top three foreign banks in India are UK-based: Standard Chartered, HSBC and Barclays.
Foreign banks can do business in India either by setting up branches or through a wholly owned subsidiary, subject to approval by the RBI.
Indian private banks can be 74% foreign owned with a 5% cap on ownership by any one entity. The Indian banking sector has introduced the use of Basel II compliance.

India's total banking assets are expected to grow to over US$1 trillion by the end of 2011.

Investment and other financial services

Market liberalisation and a huge inflow of investments into India have transformed the capital markets in the country. Across India there is a need for rapid infrastructure development meaning a greater demand for investment funds. This borrowing is unlikely to slow down as both private and public sectors strive to raise private equity to invest in social assets like hospitals, roads, ports and education amongst others.

Emerging cities are a strong driver for this as they are fast-growing centres and with the most need for modern infrastructure.

Private companies are also increasingly looking to raise venture capital in order to expand their businesses.
SME lending is a growing and yet untapped market. India's still largely rural population represents a vast segment of the population. In order to sustain growth, both government and private enterprise acknowledge that development needs to be inclusive.

Rural banking, microfinance and mobile banking therefore offer huge potential in the coming decades.

Furthermore, India's demographic composition points to growing and sustainable opportunities in pension management.

Insurance

This sector has traditionally been dominated by the state-owned Life Insurance Corporation and the General Insurance Corporation. FDI is allowed under the current cap of 26% although an upcoming bill suggests a possible increase to 49%. Foreign companies therefore require a partnership or JV to operate in the market.

Existing Indian companies involved in lending, banking, property or retail are increasingly seeking to diversify into the insurance sector. In emerging cities this can involve rural lending and insurance schemes. India offers opportunities for partnerships, either in the delivery of insurance services or to develop know-how. Life, nonlife, motor and health insurance are growing areas of opportunity, with life insurance expected to grow to US $98 billion in the next five years.

Standard Life, Prudential Life, Legal & General, and Friends Provident are some of the UK global insurance companies in India.

India presents many opportunities to UK businesses, and the drivers for growth in the financial services sector can be summarised as follows:

- Demographic: With half of India's population under the age of 30, there is potential for growth in consumer expenditure and credit. Opportunities will arise in banking and wealth management with credit expected to grow at 25% p.a.
- Regulatory: India's policies have become more investment-friendly and authorities have taken steps to reduce paperwork. Acknowledging that further investment is needed to boost growth, the government is planning further reforms particularly in banking and insurance.
- Technology: There is a greater availability and use of technology, as seen in India's high-tech stock market the widespread use of computers and mobile devices; and the

introduction of more sophisticated secure banking systems.

- Indian Enterprise: Entrepreneurs in India are increasingly looking to expand or diversify their business. To do this, they require access to venture capital and know-how. SME lending is a thriving and yet untapped segment unlikely to slow down in the near future.
- Capital expenditure: Across India there is a need for rapid infrastructure development and a greater demand for capital. To do this, both government and private industry are expected to increase borrowing.
- Economic growth: India's GDP growth of 8% or higher is in itself a strong driver for new opportunities, with forecasts set at 9.5% by 2015.

Chapter 11: Creative and Media

This broad-ranging sector comprises many different products and services. Whether e-content development, advertising services, or film dubbing, the common denominator is:

Creativity: To outline the opportunities this sector has to offer, I begin by bridging India's growing need for creative talent with UK's key competencies in the segment.

UK's Creative Industries sector is valued at over £21 billion per year; it is a dynamic sector that boasts a world class pool of talent including designers, advertisers, film production specialists, mobile content developers, games programmers and many more.

Aside from UK's unquestionable strengths in the creative business, why should UK companies turn their eyes to India and furthermore to India's emerging cities?

India's appetite for new products, technologies and services is growing rapidly. When considering India's growing middle class, it is clear that both local and foreign companies in India have a mounting need for creative talent to cater for this growing market.

The creative sector in India is not new; what is new is the fresh appetite and interest to engage with foreign partners.

The Indian media and entertainment sector is expected to grow from US $12 billion in 2009 to US $22 billion in 2014. The Indian market is very receptive to foreign expertise and easily assimilates overseas trends.

The most substantial creative sectors in India are:

- Television
- Print media
- Filmed entertainment
- Animation and gaming
- Outdoor advertising
- Music
- Design
- Publishing
- E-learning and e-publishing.

Opportunities

Based on UK's core strengths, the greatest opportunities in India's emerging cities are in:

- Marketing and brand-design consulting.
- Digital media and entertainment.
- Gaming and animation.
- Film and post-production.
- Mobile content development.
- Publishing; education content development.
- E-content.
- E-applications.

Opportunities exist for collaboration between UK based content companies and Indian developers. There are many aspects of UK's creative companies that can be replicated in the Indian market and ample room for knowledge transfer across the creative and media sector.

Two of the fastest growing Indian cities in the creative market are Pune and Bangalore, given their industrial composition, strengths and their high concentration of colleges in design, arts and engineering. While Hyderabad, home to Microsoft's India Development Centre, is emerging as a prominent destination for gaming, animation and film.

Given that UK's creative and media sector largely consists of SMEs, it becomes particularly important to understand the challenges that await them in the Indian market.

Competition from other exporting countries is strong, particularly on price, which means that identifying correct price points is essential. Also challenging could be the amount of resources required to sustain a long-term business venture in India, whether in terms of funds, staff, or time needed.

To cope with these challenges, the best course of action is to have a clear focus, conduct due diligence in your market research, and reach out to sources of support.

While the Creative & Media sector is largely open to FDI (100% in most areas), there are restrictions in print media (cap at 26%) and DTH broadcasting and FM broadcasting (cap at 20%).

There are hopes for even further liberalisation, echoed by undeniable market effervescence. Discussions have taken place at high government levels on new recommendations for raising the FDI cap on DTH broadcasting. These developments give a sense of approaching transformation.

India's Creative and Media sector is broadly speaking, open for business; a message that is resonating with other major players now actively exploring the Indian opportunity.

Marketing and brand-design consulting

India's emergence as a global player means more up-and-coming Indian companies are on the road to global growth, they will increasingly require consultancy services from world-class marketers to shape and manage their brands and global image. This is particularly the case in emerging cities where companies had previously been unaware of or unable to access international markets.

UK's leading creative businesses are very well placed to seize opportunities in this budding market of:
- Marketing
- Advertising
- Brand design
- Consulting

Digital media, gaming and animation

Many Indian companies involved in digital media and animation are interested in training, either to develop in-house resources or to provide customer training. Therefore curriculum development, e-platforms and training delivery are a budding segment.

Furthermore, Indian emerging cities offer opportunities for consulting, technology transfer, outsourcing and software R&D. There is a great interest in broadening the service range provided in India and to access new foreign technologies. In order to meet the growing domestic and foreign market for animation and digital media, Indian partners may also be open to discussing the joint setup of digital media facilities. Client referral schemes for European and Indian clients are also an area of opportunity.

Film and post production

Opportunities exist in film and post-production for UK companies keen to export their creative talent to India or to partner with existing Indian companies. India's rapid growth has not necessarily met with even growth in terms of financing.

Many post-production studios in India are actively seeking to partner with foreign companies to increase their capacity to grow.

Many Indian creative companies employ foreign talent, highlighting the scarcity of local creative staff and the resulting appetite for partnerships, JVs and acquisitions.

There are success stories of UK based companies acquiring Indian studios in mutually beneficial deals.

In addition, India's growing access to computer technology and mobile devices has opened an area of opportunity for online advertising and clips.

Mobile content development

Recently, the Indian government completed auctions for 3G service provision which will soon allow Indian mobile users to download content like music, videos and applications at faster speeds. The auction resulted in a slicing of the Indian airspace with Vodaphone, Bharti, Reliance, Aircel, Idea and Tata, in addition to state-run BSNL and MTNL, reported to become the biggest 3G providers.

This is a clear step towards market liberalisation and will result in progress for other companies, for example opportunities for strategic alliances in network delivery. Also of interest to UK companies are the ensuing opportunities for 3G-based, Value-Added Services (VAS)

Developers

Producers of short shows, clips and documentaries, music, sport, etc. Opportunities may develop faster in mature markets like the Indian metros due to their high concentration of mobile services providers but as technologies spread to emerging cities and small villages, so will the need for local content. With 15 million new mobile subscribers every month, the opportunities are enormous.

Publishing and education content

80% of India's English language book market is dominated by educational books and the rest by fiction and nonfiction.

There is an FDI cap in place for newspapers and periodicals, as well as other regulations such as approvals by the Ministry of Information and Broadcasting and safeguards for operational requirements such as a minimum number of Indian executives and editors. State governments largely produce the books used in state-run schools with some instances of partnerships with private publishers.

India presents opportunities for content development in:

- English as a first and foreign language.
- Vocational skills and accreditations.
- Subject content for the private education sector (all levels); and books for the higher education sector.

MacMillan and Pearson Education are some of the international players already in the market. In addition, India's need to educate a largely rural population will no doubt drive the market for e-learning and e-applications.

Chapter 12: Fact-file of Some of India Tier I Cities

Bangalore

Bangalore is the capital of the state of Karnataka. It is located in the south-eastern part of the state and is considered the fourth largest GDP contributor in the country after Mumbai, New Delhi and Kolkata.

Bangalore is best known for its leading IT and ITeS exports and large concentration of scientific research institutions and development centres.

City: Bangalore

State: Karnataka

Altitude: 3113 ft. above sea level

Area: 366 sq. Km

Population: 6.8 million (est.)

Average Temperature: 14° C to 33° C

Literacy: (State) 66.66%

GSDP per capita: (State) US$1,006.30 (2008-2009)
Languages: Kannada, Telugu, Tamil, Urdu, Marathi, Tulu, Kodagu, Konkani, Hindi

Bangalore enjoys a temperate climate year-round, with the rainy season stretching from August to October.

The city is one of the most diverse and multicultural cities in India, having gone through a major transformation with the influx of migrants from other Indian states and a ten-fold growth in the last decade. Today, the city is home to over 10,000 dollar-millionaires, leading to a vast concentration of wealth.

The city is well connected thanks to the newly built Bengaluru International Airport and is well-suited for hosting world-class conferences and exhibitions.

Business

Bangalore is known for its high level of literacy and education, having produced large numbers of doctors, engineers and medical technicians in the country and attracting students from across India and overseas. It is home to the Indian Institute of Science (IISc), the National Law School of India University (NLSIU), and the Indian Institute of Management, Bangalore (IIM-B) amongst many others. English is widely used as the business language in Bangalore.

The boom of the IT sector played a key role in the city's transformation. Today, Bangalore is known as the Silicon Valley of India with the state's IT and ITeS exports valued at US$16.3 billion in 2008-09.

Large businesses like Infosys and Wipro are based here. Other fast-growing sectors in Bangalore include communications, banking and insurance and business services.

Communications is one of the fastest growing sectors reporting a 26% growth rate in 08-09, while advertising is generating scores of new jobs in the city. The tertiary sector contributes more than half of the state's income in terms of GSDP.

Along with Bangalore's economic development, the influx of migrants, investment and industry have also generated an all time high in the demand for commercial space and retail real estate. This has pushed prices up and developers are now looking towards new developments in surrounding areas.

Chennai

Is India's fourth largest metropolitan city and fifth economic hub based on GDP. Formerly known as Madras, Chennai is the capital of the state of Tamil Nadu and is a major centre for music, art and culture.

Close to many cultural and natural attractions, tourism is one of its priority economic sectors with a growth rate of 11.9% in trade, hotels and restaurants. Chennai is known as the 'Gateway to South India' and has a highly skilled, English speaking workforce. The city's economy is supported by industries such as automotive, technology, healthcare, IT and ITeS, financial services and textiles.

City: Chennai

State: Tamil Nadu

Altitude: 1350m

Area: 178.20 sq. km

Population: 7.5 million (est.)

Average Temperature: 20° C – 38° C

Literacy: (State) 73.5%

GSDP per capita (State) US$1,150.90 (07-08)

Languages: Telugu, Tamil, Bengali, Punjabi, Malayalam, English, Urdu, and Kannada.
The state of Tamil Nadu is located at the southern tip of the country and has a tropical climate meaning that it is hot and humid for most of the year. Its capital, Chennai, is well connected in terms of roads, railway, ports and telecommunications.

Chennai's international airport has recently expanded its air cargo import complex and the city's port is one of the state's major sea ports handling mainly container cargo.

To counter traffic congestion, Chennai has a well-established suburban railway network, an elevated mass-rapid-transit-system and further plans for a metro rail project.

Chennai's standard of education is highly rated in the country and higher education is strong in areas such as engineering and medicine, with colleges like the Indian Institute of Technology Madras (IIT Madras), the Guindy College of Engineering, Madras Institute of Technology, Madras Medical College (MMC) and Stanley Medical College (SMC), amongst others.

Tamil Nadu has grown at a rate of 13.2% from 2001-02 to 2008-09. Economists have even predicted an increase in per capita income to reach US$17,366 by 2050.

Tamil Nadu has attracted significant FDI in recent years and government incentives have included a strong promotion of industrial clusters and Special Economic Zones (SEZs). In Chennai, SEZs are mostly dedicated to IT and ITeS, apparel and automotive.

Chennai is known worldwide as a strong exporter of woven garments and a hub for automotive manufacturing and exports. Major automotive companies with plants in or near Chennai include: Ford, Hyundai, Mitsubishi Motors, Nissan Motors, Renault-Nissan, Daimler India, BMW and locals like Ashok Leyland.

Chennai is India's second largest exporter of IT and ITeS after Bangalore. Tamil Nadu stands above the national average in wireless connectivity and has over 28 million mobile subscribers. Electronics, led by companies Dell, Nokia, Motorola, Samsung, Siemens, Sony and Foxconn, is another booming sector.

The Tamil film industry contributes significantly to the state's GSDP, with Chennai standing at the forefront of Tamil film making. As for print media, the major English dailies published in Chennai are

The Hindu, The New Indian Express, The Deccan Chronicle and The Times of India.

Banking and Financial Services are also key sectors in Chennai. Major Indian and foreign financial institutions have a presence with banks like ABN-Amro and the World Bank sustaining back office operations in the city.

Chennai's growing retail sector saw many malls opening in 2010, with even more openings planned for 2011/12. The commercial office space segment however has been hit with poor absorption and oversupply mainly in the IT sector.

Activity in residential real estate has gained momentum with major developers like Vijay Shanthi, True Value Homes, DLF, Unitech, Akshaya Homes, Prince Foundations, Dugar, Doshi and Cee Dee Yes. All now marketing residential projects at affordable prices.

Hyderabad

The state capital of Andhra Pradesh, is famous for its rich history and culture. Also famous for its leading position as producer of precious and semi-precious gems and pearls, Hyderabad is known as the "city of pearls".

The city's economy has traditionally been dominated by the service industry, however in recent years Hyderabad has diversified into other sectors such as trade, commerce, communication, IT and ITeS1.

Pharmaceuticals and biotechnology have also become a strong economic sector, with half of the top 10 pharmaceutical companies in the country based in Hyderabad as along with a number of research institutes. The emergence of IT in Hyderabad is already earning it the title as India's next Silicon Valley.

City: Hyderabad

State: Andhra Pradesh

Altitude: 536 meters above sea level

Area: 625 sq. km

Population: 7 million (est.)

Average Temperature: 15° C – 38° C

Literacy: (State) 60.5%

GSDP per capita (State) US$947 (07-08)

Languages: Telegu, English, & Hindi

Hyderabad typically has tropical weather with a hot, dry season and a wet monsoon season. The Hyderabad international airport is well connected to cities like Amsterdam, London, Chicago, Frankfurt, Kuala Lumpur, Singapore, Dubai and major Indian destinations.

The city has actively promoted itself as a prime destination for international conferences and offers state of the art hotels and convention centres. There are also plans to build an elevated mass rapid transit system.

The state of Andhra Pradesh has set an ambitious economic plan, targeting a 9% annual growth by 2012.

The government offers a number of fiscal and sector policy incentives, which include SEZs and industrial clusters to attract even further FDI.

Clusters in Hyderabad are typically in the IT and ITeS sectors, pharmaceuticals and biotech and textiles and apparel.

IT/ITeS is a booming sector in Hyderabad. The state's share of IT exports has risen steadily, supported by operational IT/ITeS SEZs in the state.

Home to Microsoft's India Development Centre which employs approximately 1,500 staff, Hyderabad is an attractive destination for IT companies and education institutions alike.

The city is also emerging as a prominent gaming and animation hub, with local companies catering mainly for outsourced work for film, commercial and games production houses in North America and Europe.

Hyderabad is home to many animation, multi-media, recording, film and post production studios:

Annapurna Studios, Padmalaya Studios, Ramoji Film City, Dataquest and music recording studios like Alap Digital are all based here.

Hyderabad's movie Industry (Tollywood) produces the largest number of movies in India and is a major contributor to the city's economy.

Two of India's most renowned universities are based in Hyderabad: Osmania University and the University of Hyderabad. In addition to other specialised institutes, they offer degrees in business, technology, legal studies and life sciences, placing Hyderabad as an important centre for learning which attracts students from all over India and overseas (Africa and Middle East).

Organised retail is a fast-growing segment in Hyderabad. There are 20 existing plus 24 upcoming malls in the city offering well-known brands. The city therefore presents opportunities for shopping centre developers and operators.

Reliance Retail opened the first "Reliance Fresh" stores in Hyderabad in 2006, selling fresh vegetables and groceries. With the boom of IT and retail in Hyderabad, real estate has also gained momentum with the value of property rising fast.

Kolkata

Is the capital of the Indian state of West Bengal. The former capital of India, it has long been considered a cultural centre thanks to its literary and artistic tradition.

Kolkata is India's third largest urban agglomeration and third largest contributor to the country's GDP. The state's main industries include: IT, apparel, tea, mineral resources, iron, steel and biotechnology.

City: Kolkata

State: West Bengal

Altitude: 42 ft. above sea level

Area: 187.33 sq km

Population: 5 million (est.); and an estimated 15 million including surrounding areas

Average: Temperature 14° C – 36° C

Literacy: (State) 68.6%

GSDP per capita (State) US$871.8 (07-08)

Languages: Bengali, Hindi, English

Kolkata has a tropical wet-and-dry climate. Located in the north-east of India, it is the commercial gateway to eastern India and Southeast Asia with links to Nepal, Bhutan and China.

Kolkata has both an international airport and a major modern port. The 'golden quadrilateral', a highway network connecting India's major cities, had been nearly completed between Kolkata-New Delhi and Kolkata-Chennai as of April 2011.

Kolkata is the main financial hub of eastern India, having attracted FDI inflows for US$1.3 billion (Kolkata region) during 2000-09, according to the Department of Industrial Policy and Promotion.

The city also offers lower costs of operation compared to other cities like New Delhi, Bangalore, Chennai, Hyderabad or Mumbai. Major Indian companies headquartered in Kolkata include: Bata India, ITC Limited, Birla Corporation, Domodar Valley Corporation and Allahabad Bank.

Kolkata's workforce is highly talented and English is largely used as the language of business. There are 18 universities in the state of West Bengal, and Kolkata is home to renowned institutions such as the Indian Institute of Management Calcutta (IIM-C), and the Indian Institute of Technology in Kharagpur (IIT-KGP).

Local talent has been a driver for the IT industry's boom in the city with IT businesses setting up in the city to search for home-grown talent that has long powered the IT industry in cities like Hyderabad or Bangalore.

The state has put forward incentives for the IT sector, developing a number of growth centres in Rajarhat, greater Kolkata. As a result, Kolkata's IT sector is growing at an annual rate of 70% and boasts a strong list of companies with offices in the city including: Genpact, Cognizant Technology Solutions, Tata Consultancy Services, IBM Global Services, Wipro and Siemens Information Systems.

Kolkata's infrastructure and suitable agro-climatic conditions also support a prominent tea industry with an important presence of tea producers, traders and exporters based in the city.

The city is teeming with small and micro businesses from hawkers along the footpath to small retailers in every nook and corner of the suburban landscape. It is estimated that roadside hawking alone generated business worth nearly GBP100 million in 2009. Unfortunately, demand for retail space has not grown as expected and malls are now being transformed into office space.

West Bengal is a state with abundant mineral resources. Its iron ore deposits make it a favoured destination for the steel industry. SEZ in the city of Kolkata mainly operate in garments, engineering, IT/ITeS and biotechnology.

Pune

Is the second largest city in the state of Maharashtra and is located 150 km east of Mumbai, the state's capital.

The city of Pune is a renowned tourist destination, home to many historical monuments, palaces and museums.

Pune is a strong player in the engineering and automotive industries, food and agro and IT/ITeS.

City: Pune

State: Maharashtra

Altitude: 560 meters above sea level

Area: 451 sq. km

Population: 3.5 million (est.)

Average Temperature: 15° C – 36° C

Literacy (State) 76.9%

GSDP per capita (State) US$1,369.90 (07-08)

Languages Marathi, Hindi and English

Pune has a tropical wet and dry climate with three distinct seasons: Summer (March-May), monsoon (June-October) and winter (November-January).

This majorly industrial city has boomed in recent years thanks to the establishment of several SEZs and industrial clusters in: IT/ITeS, hardware and software, electronics, pharmaceuticals and biotech and food and agro.

Companies like Frito Lay and Coca Cola are located in Pune.

The city has received considerable investment for the development of its urban infrastructure. For example, the state of Maharashtra is planning a 1,000 MW power plant to exclusively meet Pune's growing electricity demands.

The Mumbai-Pune expressway, a 93 Km. 6-lane highway, connects the two cities with a journey of approximately two hours and Pune's Lohegaon Airport operates international flights.

Pune is an important education hub, with its schools and colleges known for their quality of education. Some of the most popular educational institutions are: Symbiosis International University, Pune University, Bharati Vidyapeeth, Institute of Armament Technology and Dr.D.Y. Patil University.

Pune is a key supplier and resource centre for the entertainment industry based in Maharashtra and Mumbai's widely popular Hindi film industry. The renowned Film and Television Institute of India (FTII), one of the oldest and finest institutes in the field of training in film making and television programme production, is located in Pune.

The state of Maharashtra accounts for 38% of the country's automobile manufacturing and Pune is one of its major production centres. Companies like Bajaj Auto Limited, Volkswagen India, Daimler Chrysler Limited, Tata Motors and John Deere all have manufacturing facilities in Pune.

Furthermore, the engineering sector in Pune is highly diversified with an important output of engineering goods, machinery and automotive parts.

Key engineering companies such as Bharat Forge Limited, Cummins Engines, Bosch and Honeywell are also located in Pune.

Pune's IT and electronics sector has grown considerably, largely due to the many industrial clusters and SEZs dotted around the city. Major software companies have operating and BPO centres, back-end support services, R&D and captive facilities in Pune: Accenture, IBM, Symantec, Infosys, Tata's TCS, Wipro and HSBC amongst many others.

The city's retail sector is expected to witness a 51% compounded growth over the next five years, one of the most active markets in western India. Pune has boosted the real estate sector with a growing demand for commercial space and luxury housing complexes.

Chapter 13: Preparing to Export to India

Visitors to India are advised to undertake as much market research and planning as possible, prior to their visit. It would also be helpful to consider India as a long-term market as usually more than one visit is necessary to establish appropriate contacts and gain market credibility.

What companies should consider when doing business in India

The Indian balance of payments crisis in the early 1990s was the spur for a series of far-reaching economic reforms. These reforms have transformed the Indian economy and helped deliver average growth of some 8.5% a year over the last five years. This growth has been underpinned by increasing private sector activity in services and manufacturing, particularly in BPO activities and the IT, bio-technology, pharmaceutical and automotive sectors.

There is a danger that the impressive economic growth rates enjoyed by India over recent years and required to help successfully absorb the new entrants into the labour market will stall without further reform.

Reducing barriers to trade and investment is key but tackling the problems posed by corruption, excessive bureaucracy and poor infrastructure are important challenges ahead. Reforms to the tightly regulated employment market will also be needed if the economy is to generate enough jobs to readily absorb the new labour market entrants.

Gateways/Locations

Key areas for business is perhaps more accurate to describe India as a collection of linked markets rather than simply one large market. This is important to appreciate because successful business in India is best achieved by having a series of regional business plans in place. Ideally, these should address the distinctiveness of India's regions, the challenges they pose and the actual opportunities they present for your firm.

Accessing those opportunities will, amongst other things, require a coherent strategy for tackling the linguistic and cultural differences, varying customer preferences and expectations and the distribution requirements particular to each region.

At present, approximately 30 per cent of India's population of 1.2billion live in some 200 major towns and cities, the remainder are classed as rural dwellers.

The key cities are: Mumbai (population 16.5m); Kolkata (13.5m); New Delhi (13m); Chennai (6.5m); Bangalore (5.7m); Hyderabad (5.5m); Ahmedabad (5m) and Pune (4m).

The significant distances separating these cities is compounded by a creaking transport infrastructure and the challenges these pose for effective supply and distribution should not be underestimated. Despite significant reductions in import duty rates since the early 1990s, tariff rates in India continue to be comparatively high; from a peak rate of 350 per cent in 1991 to 150% in 2010; and the current average rate of 10 per cent masks considerable differences.

High tariff levels may impact upon your competitiveness initially but tariffs remain on a downward trend. Furthermore, India's commitment to the WTO and its stated desire to tackle IPR enforcement are encouraging signs that the market for foreign goods and services will continue to grow.

Chapter 14: Market Entry and Start up Considerations

The key factors to consider when drawing-up a business plan for tackling India include managing distribution and sales channels, labelling and documentation conformity, realistic pricing and marketing options and ensuring protection of intellectual property rights.

As mentioned earlier in this book, consider approaching India's markets on a regional basis. It is worth noting that language, caste and religion remain major influences over social and political organisation in India. These differences matter and one region is not very much like another. Focus on one area or region at a time to see what works and what doesn't.

Sound local advice and assistance will be crucial and good local representatives essential. You may find that it is best to appoint a series of Agents or Distributors based on their local reach and impact rather than one who might not be able to adequately cover more than one region.

As elsewhere, before appointing an Agent or Distributor it is important to undertake a thorough evaluation exercise. Look closely at your potential partner's local business reputation and industry standing, its financial resources and credit worthiness, regional coverage and marketing ability. A good, local representative will be keen to help you grow your business and have the resources available to do so.

This is particularly important in terms of warehousing and distribution. In recent years, firms specialising in distribution and logistics have expanded their business across India considerably and there are now many Clearing and Forwarding agents to chose from.

For firms who wish to establish a deeper business operation in India, several options are available, namely, creating Liaison, Branch or Project offices or establishing a Joint Venture business. There are key differences between what activities these entities are allowed to undertake.

Liaison offices cannot engage directly in commercial activity in India. Such offices primarily exist to co-ordinate marketing and business development functions.

A Branch office is allowed to conduct business in India and to repatriate profits to the parent company after payment of any due taxes.

A Project office is a similar entity but usually established for the purpose of undertaking a specific, time-limited project awarded to the parent company.

Chapter 15: Import Regulations

Competent legal advice should be sought when considering Customs and Regulations India's current regulations are guided by the Export Import Policy of 2002-2007. Imports are permitted in most cases without a license but exceptions exist where items are imported only under license or where imports are allowed only through a government-owned entity.

Custom duties are levied on imports of goods into India. This is governed by the Customs Act 1962 and the Customs Tariff Act 1975. The Harmonised System for customs classifications is used and Customs Duty on imports comprises of the following elements: Basic Customs Duty levied as either

i)   A specific rate based, by unit, on the item, or more commonly.

ii)   Ad-valorem, based on the assessable value. Additional Customs Duty levied on the assessed value of goods plus Basic Customs Duty. Goods that fall into this category generally tend to have similar, locally-manufactured competitors. This duty helps protect domestic industry from cheap imports.

Special Additional Customs Duty, levied on all items; currently at the rate of 4 per cent of the basic and the excise duty on all imports.

Anti-Dumping Duty; levied, from time to time, on specified goods imported from specified countries.

Customs Education Cess; currently levied at the rate of 3 per cent of Basic Customs Duty and Additional Customs Duty.

In addition, a 1 per cent Customs Handling Fee is imposed on all imports. This is in addition to the applied customs duty. Indian customs regulations allow for the temporary import of goods into India.

For goods that are imported for a temporary period and exported out of India a drawback of part of the customs duty is possible. In addition, General Exemption 14 of the Customs Tariff allows, subject to conditions, the import of goods for use or display at exhibitions and trade fairs. India adheres to the Customs Valuation Agreement of the multilateral trade negotiations held under the Tokyo GATT round.

Import duties in India included both specific duties (i.e. rates specified without reference to value of the imported goods) and ad valorem (i.e. rates specified as a percent of the value of the imported goods). Ad valorem duties are gradually replacing specific duties. There has been a consistent decline in the import tariff over the past few years.

The peak customs duty on non-agricultural goods was reduced to 15 percent from 20 percent in 2006. The customs duties on selected capital goods and parts have been reduced to below 15 per cent, to 10 per cent in some cases and to 5 per cent in some others. The Indian customs tariff can be found at the following.

website http://www.cbec.gov.in/customs/cst-0910/cst-main.htm

India's legislative and administrative procedure on customs valuation are consistent with the GATT customs valuation code and custom tariffs are levied on the CIF value of imports or the transaction value of the goods. Thus import duty is levied on the price that the buyer pays to the seller. For the purpose of valuation of imported goods, additional costs and services (such as royalties, license fees or any amount paid by the buyer as a condition of sale of goods) the value of which is not included in the transaction value may be included.

Indian customs and central excise laws contain the provision of advance tax rulings to guide investors and exporters to India on tax liability in India, and on the customs and excise duty implications on various transactions. The provisions enable manufacturers and importers to obtain in advance a binding ruling on issues which might arise in determining their tax liabilities. However, there is no mechanism to administer this provision.

Chapter 16: Income Tax Law

The Income Tax law provides for deducting tax before payment of various types of income including salaries, dividends, interest on securities, insurance commissions, payments to contractors and sub-contractors and rental income from land or buildings.

This is called Withholding Tax. Withholding taxes are offset against gross tax liability. Tax is also deducted at source on payments to non-residents or foreigners.

Different thresholds and rates apply depending on the type on income. Rates of withholding tax are specified in the annual Finance Act. India has agreed Double Taxation Avoidance Treaties with several countries, including the UK that specifies withholding tax rates applicable to certain types of outbound payments.

Tax rates applicable in India under the India/UK DTA are as follows:

- Dividends other than those exempted under the Indian Income Tax Act 15% not exceeding 15 percent of the gross amount of Dividend.
- Interest: if paid to a bank 10% not to exceed 10% of the gross amount of the interest; if paid to others; not exceed 15 percent of the gross amount of the interest
- Royalties and fees for technical services would be taxable in the country of source at the following rates:

- o In cases where rental of equipment and services is provided along with know-how and technical fees 10%; not to exceed 10 percent of the gross amount of such royalties and fees for technical services.
  - o Any other case-
- During the first five years of agreement, if the payer is Government or specified organisation 15% and in other cases 20%
- Subsequent years, in all cases 15% further, income of Government and certain institutions will be exempt from taxation in the country of source. The Income Tax law also provides a system of advance rulings to non-residents, enabling them to obtain in advance of any actual transactions a binding ruling on issues which could arise in determining their tax liabilities.

Chapter 17: Imports Documentation and Standard

Importers are required to submit to Customs an Import Declaration noting the value of the imported goods. This needs to be accompanied by an Invoice (Ex-Factory), a Freight Certificate and all Insurance Certificates. If an Import Licence is required, that too will also need to accompany the documentation submitted to Customs. Although Indian Customs now operate 24 hours a day, cargo clearances can be subject to delays and such delays lead, of course, to increased demurrage charges.

Labelling and Packaging Regulations

Labelling requirements are an important element to consider when exporting to India. All containers and packages must carry appropriate information depending upon the consignment.

Indian Customs generally ensure that imported items have the legally required information before these are allowed to enter the local retail market. The Ministry of Commerce issued a formal Notification in November 2000 which stated that all pre-packaged commodities, intended for direct retail sale, imported into India must carry the following declarations on the label:

- The name and address of the registered importer.

- The generic or common name of the commodity packed for import.
- Net quantity in terms of standard unit of weights and measurement. (All units of weight and measurements to be in metric.)
- The month and year of packaging in which the item is manufactured, packed or imported, and
- The maximum retail sales price at which the goods, in packaged form, may be sold to the end consumer. The maximum retail sales price is meant to include all taxes and all charges related to freight forwarding, re-packing, advertising, commission payable to dealers etc.

These declarations may be printed, on the package, in English or Hindi. Printing on a label securely affixed to the package or on an additional wrapper containing the imported package is also permitted. Compliance of these requirements needs to be ensured before consignments are cleared by Customs in India.

Slightly different arrangements apply to pre-packaged commodities such as raw materials or components that need to undergo further processing before they are sold to consumers. It is important to remember that consignments to India should be strongly packed. Packages may receive heavy handling and be left in the open air for longer than anticipated.

Standards

The Bureau of Indian Standards (BIS) is the organisation responsible for the development of national standards. These national standards are generally in-line with international norms and most are harmonized with ISO standards. However, imports of some 109 products are subject to compliance with specified Indian quality standards. To remain compliant with the law, manufacturers of these products must obtain certification from the Bureau of Indian Standards before exporting such goods to India.

The list includes food preservatives and additives, milk powder, certain electrical appliances, some types of gas cylinders, cement and certain batteries. These products must be tested and certified by BIS in India although BIS does offer pre-certification subject to production inspections.

Chapter 18: Intellectual Property Rights

India is one of Britain's priority overseas markets.

If you plan to do business in India, or if you are already trading there, it is essential to know how to use, guard and enforce the rights you have over the intellectual property (IP) that you or your business own.

This book explains about IP in general, and gives guidance on how to apply these principles in the Indian market. It describes the issues you may face with IP infringement in India, offers advice on how you can effectively tackle these, and provides links to sources of further help.

What are intellectual property rights?

Intellectual property (IP) is a term referring to a brand, invention, design or other kind of creation, which a person or business has legal rights over. Almost all businesses own some form of IP, which could be a business asset.

India has been a member of the World Trade Organisation (WTO) since 1995. This requires member nations to establish intellectual property (IP) laws whose effect is in line with minimum standards. As a result, there should be few major differences between India's laws and those of other developed countries.

To enjoy most types of intellectual property (IP) rights in India, you should register them.

For patents, individual registrations must be made in India, but for rights other than industrial designs you can apply under the terms of the Patent Cooperation Treaty, which is usually easier and quicker.

For trade-marks, you should register them within India.

For copyright, no registration is required but registering copyrights with the copyright authorities is advisable.

'Priority rights' under the Paris Convention can help in the local registration of trade-marks, designs and patents by allowing rights previously registered elsewhere to become effective in India, if filed within a time limit.

India is a signatory to the Agreement on Trade-Related Intellectual Property Rights (TRIPS).

The TRIPS lays down minimum standards for protection and enforcement of intellectual property rights (IPR) in WTO Member countries which are required to promote effective and adequate protection of intellectual property rights with a view to reducing distortions and impediments to international trade.

The obligations under the TRIPS Agreement relate to provision of minimum standard of protection within the member countries legal systems and practices. IPR in India is well established at all levels; statutory, administrative, and judicial it covers the key areas, mentioned below.

Copyright

Copyright - this protects written or published works such as books, songs, films, web content and artistic works.
India is a signatory to the Berne Convention on copyright, however, it may be a good idea to register your copyright as doing so may help to prove ownership if there are criminal proceedings against infringers.

In most cases though, registration is not necessary to maintain a copyright infringement claim in India. Registration is made, in person or via a representative, with the Copyright Office.

Internet piracy of films, music, books and software is particularly severe in India.

As I mentioned earlier copyright is the legal right granted to an author, composer, playwright, publisher, or distributor to exclusive publication, production, sale, or distribution of a literary, musical, dramatic, or artistic work.

The Indian Copyright Act is compliant with most international conventions and treaties in the field of copyrights.

India is a member of the World Intellectual Property Organisation (WIPO), the Berne Union for Protection of Literary and Artistic Works, the Nairobi Treaty of the Olympic Symbol and the Universal Copyright Convention (UCC).

This means that any person that enjoys a copyright in any of these convention countries automatically gets statutory copyright protection in India. Though India is not a member of the Rome Convention of 1961, the Copyright Act, 1957 is fully compliant with the Rome Convention provisions. India's copyright law as laid down in the Copyright Act of 1957 was replaced by the Copyright (Amendment) Act of 1999. The Act vests copyright in the authors on creation of their works and require no registration.

Registration provides prima facie evidence of a copyright's validity and is advisable. The Act covers computer programs, satellite broadcasting and digital technology. The Act provides for copyright enforcement.

A person whose copyright is infringed may sue for civil relief, and may even institute criminal proceedings for infringement in certain cases.

The Government has taken some measures over the past two years to strengthen and streamline the enforcement of copyrights. These include establishment of a Copyright Enforcement Advisory Council and special policy cells to deal with cases relating to violation of copyrights.

Copyright abuse and piracy is widespread and IPR enforcement is weak. It is therefore important that the rights' holder should develop a robust IPR strategy before entering the Indian market.

Patents

Patents - this protects commercial inventions, e.g. a new business, product or process.

India's Patents Act of 1970 and 2003 Patent Rules set out the law concerning patents. As in the UK, there is no provision for utility model patents.

The regulatory authority for patents is the Patent Registrar within the department of the Controller General of Patents, Designs and Trade Marks, which is part of India's Ministry of Commerce and Industry. Patents are valid for 20 years from the date of filing an application, subject to an annual renewal fee.

India's patent law operates under the 'first to file' principle - that is, if two people apply for a patent on an identical invention, the first one to file the application will be awarded the patent.

Following TRIPS, the basic obligation in the area of patents is that, inventions in all branches of technology whether products or processes are patentable if these meet the three tests of being new, involve an inventive step and are capable of an industrial application.

The minimum term of protection is 20 years counted from the date of filing. As per India's TRIPS obligation, the Patents (Amendment) Act 2005 strengthened pre-grant opposition procedures. It made a provision for hearing at the pre-grant opposition stage in the rules. It also extended the timeline for pre-grant opposition to six months. An important provision of the Act is on compulsory licensing (CL).

LDCs with no or insufficient pharmaceutical manufacturing capacities can import patented drugs from India under paragraph 6 mechanism provided in the Doha Ministerial Declaration without issuing a CL to an Indian firm.
Importing countries can do so by authorising or notifying its requirements.

It is worth noting that India follows a patent registration system that gives priority to the first inventor to file an application. It is therefore crucial that applicants for patents in India file as early as possible irrespective of when they plan to begin using the product in India. The rights' holder should therefore seek appropriate legal advice before launching in India.

Designs

Designs - this protects designs, such as drawings or computer models.

The laws governing designs are the Designs Act 2000 and the Designs Rules 2001. Designs are valid for a maximum of ten years, renewable for a further five years.

Trade-marks

Trade-marks - this protects signs, symbols, logos, words or sounds that distinguish your products and services from those of your competitors.

Trade Marks have been defined as any sign, or any combination of signs capable of distinguishing goods or services of one undertaking from that of other undertakings. Such distinguishing marks constitute protectable subject matter under the provisions of the TRIPS Agreement.

Trademarks, once registered, are valid for seven years. Stringent penalties are imposed for falsifying a trademark or selling goods to which a false trademark is applied.

There is no restriction on use of foreign-owned trademarks for goods sold in India. A new Trademarks Act was approved by Parliament in 1999 replacing the Trade and Merchandised Marks Act of 1958, and provided a new basis for protection of trademarks in India. The new Act provided statutory protection to service marks, and simplified the definition of what constitutes an infringement of a registered trademark or service-mark. It also increased the duration of registration and its subsequent registration from seven to ten years.

India's trade-mark laws consist of the 1999 Trade Marks Act and the Trade Marks Rules of 2002, which became effective in 2003.

The regulatory authority for patents is the Trade Mark Registrar within the Department of the Controller General of Patents, Designs and Trade Marks. The police now have more robust powers in enforcing trade mark law; including the ability to search premises and seize goods suspected of being counterfeit without a warrant. But these powers are tempered by the requirement for the police to seek the Trade Mark Registrar's opinion on the registration of the mark before taking action. This adds to the delay and may result in counterfeit goods being removed or sold.

Trade names also constitute a form of trade mark in India, with protection, irrespective of existing trade names, for those wishing to trade under their own surname. Because of the widespread practice of 'cybersquatting' - the registration in bad faith of marks by third parties registering domain names for certain well known marks in order to sell them to the original rights owners

It is advisable for rights owners to register their domain names in India as trade-marks as soon as possible.

Registration takes up to two years. A trade-mark in India is valid for ten years and can be renewed thereafter indefinitely for further ten-year periods.

IP can be either registered or unregistered

With unregistered IP, you automatically have legal rights over your creation. Unregistered forms of IP include copyright, unregistered design rights, common law trade-marks and database rights, confidential information and trade secrets.

With registered IP, you will have to apply to an authority, such as the Intellectual Property Office in the UK, to have your rights recognised. If you do not do this, others are free to exploit your creations. Registered forms of IP include patents, registered trade-marks and registered design rights.

International considerations

India has been a World Trade Organisation (WTO) member since 1995. WTO member nations must include some IP protection in their national laws. This means that if you are doing business with India, you will find some similarity between local IP law and enforcement procedures, and those in force in the UK.

Treaties and reciprocal agreements

India is also a signatory to the following international IP agreements:
- The Paris Convention - under this, any person from a signatory state can apply for a patent or trade mark in any other signatory state, and will be given the same enforcement rights and status as a national of that country would be.

- The Berne Convention - under this, each member state recognises the copyright of authors from other member states in the same way as the copyright of its own nationals.
- The Patent Cooperation Treaty - this is a central system for obtaining a 'bundle' of national patent applications in different jurisdictions through a single application

India is not a signatory to the Madrid Protocol, which allows a bundle of national trade mark registrations in different jurisdictions to be made through a single application. It is also not a signatory to the Hague Agreement, which allows the protection of designs in multiple countries through a single filing.

Enforcing IP rights in India

IP rights can be enforced by bringing actions to the civil courts or through criminal prosecution. India's laws governing all forms of IP set out procedures for both civil and criminal proceedings, as does the Competition Act.

A disadvantage of civil litigation is that you are unlikely to recover large damages, and punitive damages against an infringer are rare. Damages are routinely awarded in cases of copyright piracy and trade mark infringement, less so in patent cases.

As in other countries, the Indian government brings actions in criminal cases, although in most cases actions follow complaints to magistrates or police authorities by rights owners. Criminal proceedings

94

against infringers carry the prospect of much harsher remedies, including fines and imprisonment.

Mediation or negotiation with an infringer can also be effective as an alternative form of dispute resolution. The Civil Procedure Code provides for a formal mediation process.

Self-help considerations

There are various things you can do to make it harder in general for infringers to copy your product. For example, you could:

- Think about the design of your product, and how easy it would be for somebody to reproduce it without seeing your original designs.
- When you hire staff, have effective IP-related clauses in employment contracts. Also make sure you educate your employees on IP rights and protection.
- Have sound physical protection and destruction methods for documents, drawings, tooling, samples, machinery etc.
- Make sure there are no 'leakages' of packaging that might be used by counterfeiters to pass off fake product.
- Check production over-runs to make sure that genuine product is not being sold under a different name.

Potential problems faced in India and how to deal with them

India's intellectual property (IP) legislation covers every significant aspect of the protection of IP. The regulations relating to all forms of IP have been amended or reissued in recent years, mainly in response to India's accession to the World Trade Organisation in 1995.

Although Indian IP law is thorough and generally comparable with European IP laws, there are still significant concerns over IP enforcement. A major cause for concern in enforcement is bureaucratic delay, with a backlog of cases at both the civil and criminal courts. This means that cases can run for five years or more. There is also a lack of transparency, particularly at a local level.

A significant feature of the IP environment in India is the large number of small players infringing IP rights. This means that seizures tend to be small, which requires a sustained and financially draining effort in order to make an impact.

An advantage for UK businesses operating in India is that the legal system is based on common law, as in the UK, so the fundamental processes are familiar.

Avoiding problems

The most important way to avoid problems when defending IP rights in India is to be prepared. To make sure that you can anticipate any potential issues, you should:

- Take advice from Indian IP rights experts.
- Consult publications and websites on Indian IP rights and protection in general.
- Carry out risk assessment and due diligence checks on any organisations and individuals you deal with.
- Take professional advice from other experts, e.g. lawyers, local diplomatic posts, Chambers of Commerce and the UK India Business Council.
- Talk to other businesses already doing similar business in India.
- Consult agents, distributors and suppliers on how best to safeguard your rights.
- Check with trade mark or patent attorneys to see whether there have been previous registrations of your own marks, or other IP, in India.
- Stick to familiar business methods; don't be tempted to do things differently because you're trading in a different country.

Who should take responsibility for your IP protection?

You should make sure that everyone in your business takes some responsibility for IP protection. Many businesses depend on the integrity of their IP, and it can often be one of their most valuable assets. So it should be given proper attention by both managements and employees, as well as other businesses that you have relationships with.

It may be sensible to nominate a manager to have particular responsibility for understanding and protecting your IP rights. In businesses with legal departments, a legally-trained manager would be a good choice.

Top tips for IP protection in India

The most important things you can do to protect your IP rights in India are:

- Stick to your normal business instincts.
- Do as much as you can to prevent Infringements in the first place; prevention is better than the cure.
- Assess the risks of the market and make preparations.
- Take self-help measures to protect your IP
- Make sure everyone in your business values its IP, including you.
- Register your IP rights.
- Create good relationships with organisations that can help you.
- Consider mediation before defensive action.

Where to get intellectual property help in India

Whether you're resident in and doing business in India, or trading internationally with the country, there are a number of professional organisations that can offer you advice and support.

The British High Commission, New Delhi offers advice on working with India, including details of cultural relations. It provides a full range of diplomatic, consular and business-related services.

- The UK India Business Council (UKIBC) helps and supports British businesses to trade with India.
- UK Trade & Investment India has a range of online information on doing business in India.
- The European Union (EU) Chamber of Commerce in India helps and supports contacts between businesses based in EU member states and India.
- Local law firms in India can offer you legal advice and services specific to your business.

Geographical Indications

Geographical indications are defined as indications which identify a good as originating in the territory of a Member, or a region or locality in that territory, where a given quality, reputation or other characteristic of the good is essentially attributable to its geographic origin.

The TRIPS Agreement contains a general obligation that parties shall provide the legal means for interested parties to prevent the use of any means in the designation or presentation of a good that indicates or suggests that the good in question originates in a geographical area other than the true place of origin in a manner which misleads the public as to the geographical origin of the goods.

There is no obligation under the Agreement to protect geographical indications, which are not protected in their country, or origin or which have fallen into disuse in that country. A new law for the protection of geographical indications, viz. the Geographical Indications of Goods (Registration and the Protection) Act, 1999 was passed by the Parliament. Industrial Design - Industrial Design is an applied art whereby the aesthetics and usability of products may be improved.

Design aspects specified by the Industrial designer may include the overall shape of the object, the location of details with respect to one another, colours, texture.

Obligations on industrial designs are that independently created designs that are new or original shall be protected. Individual governments have been given the option to exclude from protection, designs dictated by technical or functional considerations, as against aesthetic consideration, which constitutes the coverage of industrial designs.

The right accruing to the right holder is the right to prevent third parties not having his consent from making, selling or importing articles being or embodying a design, which is a copy or substantially a copy of the protected design when such acts are undertaken for commercial purposes.

The duration of protection is to be not less than 10 years. A new designs law repealing and replacing the Designs Act, 1911 was passed in 2000. IP rights are territorial, that is they only give protection in the countries where they are granted or registered. If you are thinking about trading internationally then you should consider registering your IP rights abroad.

Chapter 19: Business Etiquette

Language and Culture

While the universal language of a smile and gracious nod may result in an instant warmth in India, the most common social courtesy is greeting with hands folded as in a prayer, which is known as namaste.

Women should generally be greeted with folded hands; shaking hands, except in westernised circles, should be avoided. However, when men greet each other, they usually shake hands.

Etiquette requires the use of the right hand when giving or receiving. It is a prevalent business practice to exchange visiting cards. In large cities, business meetings and entertainment are conducted as in Western countries. Although Indians are known for their hospitality towards strangers, it is not customary for business associates to be entertained at home.

Women business travellers

Women in the business community in India are greeted with a high degree of respect. There is no discrimination and they are free to carry on their day to day business activities. Modes of address for business and official contacts are addressed as Mr/ Mrs/Ms or Sri/Smt (Srimati) by surname. Superiors are often spoken to as "sir" or "madam". Use of the first name is not common. Business superiors and those senior in age are almost always addressed formally.

Translation and interpreter services

There is no real need for an interpreter and a translation service as English is widely spoken in all circles. However, in cases of difficulty, there is always someone readily available to assist.

Chapter 20: What are the Challenges?

There is a danger that the impressive economic growth rates enjoyed by India over recent years and required to help successfully absorb the new entrants into the labour market will stall without further reform.

Reducing barriers to trade and investment is key but tackling the problems posed by corruption, excessive bureaucracy and poor infrastructure are important challenges ahead. Reforms to the tightly regulated employment market will also be needed if the economy is to generate enough jobs to readily absorb the new labour market entrants.

Despite significant reductions in import duty rates since the early 1990s, tariff rates in India continue to be comparatively high, from a peak rate of 350 per cent in 1991 to 150% in 2010 and the current average rate of 10 per cent masks considerable differences. High tariff levels may impact upon your competitiveness initially but tariffs remain on a downward trend.

Furthermore, India's commitment to the WTO and its stated desire to tackle IPR enforcement are encouraging signs that the market for foreign goods and services will continue to grow.

Distribution and Logistics

It is perhaps more accurate to describe India as a collection of linked markets rather than simply one large market. This is important to appreciate because successful business in India is best achieved by having a series of regional business plans in place.

Ideally, these should address the distinctiveness of India's regions, the challenges they pose and the actual opportunities they present for your firm. Accessing those opportunities will, amongst other things, require a coherent strategy for tackling the linguistic and cultural differences, varying customer preferences and expectations and the distribution requirements particular to each region.

The key factors to consider when drawing-up a Business Plan for tackling India include managing distribution and sales channels, labelling and documentation conformity, realistic pricing and marketing options and ensuring protection of intellectual property rights.

As mentioned earlier in this book, consider approaching India's markets on a regional basis. It is worth noting that language, caste and religion remain major influences over social and political organisation in India. These differences matter and one region is not very much like another.

Focus on one area or region at a time to see what works and what doesn't. Sound local advice and assistance will be crucial and good local representatives essential. You may find that it is best to appoint a series of Agents or Distributors based on their local reach and impact rather than one who might not be able to adequately cover more than one region. Before appointing an Agent or Distributor it is important to undertake a thorough evaluation exercise.

Look closely at your potential partner's local business reputation and industry standing, its financial resources and credit worthiness, regional coverage and marketing ability. A good, local representative will be keen to help you grow your business and have the resources available to do so. This is particularly important in terms of warehousing and distribution.

The majority of India's population are rural dwellers and consumer research suggests that the market for goods and services in rural India is growing as consumption patterns change and disposable incomes rise. Increased media penetration, particularly by television, of rural areas has helped drive this change by stimulating demand. Demands that simply did not exist 15 to 20 years ago. However, do not underestimate the challenges of serving these rural consumers. Poor infrastructure poses real distribution challenges.

With some 500 million people under the age of 25, India's growing population appears to present limitless opportunities for foreign firms. However, it is important to be realistic about the scale of the actual opportunities that exist for your product or service. Indian consumers are very price sensitive and while some consumers appreciate the quality vs. cost trade-off, many happily sacrifice quality for competitive pricing.

Simply switching products and pricing strategies from another market are highly unlikely to work in India. Detailed market research will be required.

Ensure that your goods, including packaging and marketing, are adapted to local preferences and tastes. A good local representative will therefore be an invaluable resource.

Regulatory Transparency Politicians, bureaucrats and law enforcement officials often wield significant discretionary power and notable abuses have been brought to light. Several high-profile prosecutions in recent years have helped highlight that the legal framework for fighting corruption exists although enforcement is often weak and responses vary from State to State. The Indian Prime Minister has targeted corruption as a barrier to India's efforts to 'march ahead as a nation' and the Indian Government regularly blacklists companies known to offer bribes from bidding for defence contracts.

Corruption is well entrenched in India and pervades many aspects of daily life. Corruption is often cited as a barrier to the effective development of the private sector and poses business risks that require pro-active management in the form of regular due diligence exercises and up-to-date risk strategies.

Procurement practices often lack transparency and are usually coupled with a significant bureaucratic burden. These risks require careful management.

Organised Crime

A number of British companies have been attracted by potentially lucrative business offers in India but there have been examples of fraud carried out using private data subsequently shared between the British and Indian companies. There have also been some specific examples of rogue Call Centres in India inappropriately using financial data acquired legitimately from their UK business partner. I therefore always recommend you research the market as best you can to understand any differences to the business environment in the UK and conduct basic due diligence before making any financial commitments (eg. checking that your Indian counterpart is a properly registered business and has a good reputation).

When considering doing business with Indian firms unfamiliar to you, it is worth bearing in mind the following:

- An offer 'too good to be true' may, in fact, be just that.
- Verify the data of your business partner, make appropriate due diligence checks.
- Increase your vigilance when using e-commerce.
- When making purchases, use secure payment instruments. When selling, secure the payment before delivery of the products.

Chapter 21: Risks of Doing Business in India

Below are information on key security and political risks which UK businesses may face when operating in India.

The Indian Constitution provides a system of parliamentary and cabinet government both at the centre and in the states.

India has a troubled relationship with its neighbour Pakistan, leading to at least three wars since the two countries achieved independence in 1947. Since 2004, India and Pakistan have had several rounds of negotiations and set up a 'Composite Dialogue' aimed at settling all bilateral issues, including Kashmir. The Composite Dialogue remains suspended following the terrorist attacks in Mumbai in November 2008. Bilateral talks resumed in February 2010 but have made little progress yet.

India also has a complex relationship with China, with whom it shares a long, contested border. The two countries fought a short war in 1964 and have been unable to settle their respective territorial claims since then.

India has a robust parliamentary tradition, an independent judiciary, professional armed forces, a vibrant civil society, and free and outspoken media. India has signed and ratified all of the major

International Treaties and Covenants on Human Rights except the Convention Against Torture, which it signed in 1997. There has been progress on human rights in a number of areas, including on women's rights and an important recent development for child rights has been the adoption of the 2009 Right to Education Act guaranteeing free, compulsory and quality education for children aged 6-14 years which came into effect on 1 April 2010. But implementation of legislation varies from state to state and awareness of human rights issues is inconsistent. For example, there continue to be reports of the use of child labour, particularly in the textile industry.

More information on political risk, including political demonstrations, is available in FCO Travel Advice where you will also find details of LOCATE, the FCO's on-line registration service should you want the nearest High Commission to keep you informed of a crisis or similar emergency.

Growth prospects remain strong with First Quarter results showing 7.8% growth over the same period last year underlining the broad strength in manufacturing and services. However, inflation at 8.9% is a concern. The Central Bank has gradually raised interest rates - nine times in 15 months to stand at 7.25% at the time of writing this book; in an effort to cool inflationary pressures. The Government is predicting a fall to 6% based on this year's regular monsoon/good crops and an associated easing of food price pressures.

The Indian government is also watching the widening of current account deficit, which has risen above 3% of GDP, and the sustainability of capital inflows. India has a trade deficit of near 10% (of GDP) and is especially sensitive to oil prices, with energy related imports 7.5% of GDP. Unlike other large manufacturing exporters, India relies on a combination of service exports, remittances from overseas workers and foreign capital to plug the trade gap and build its foreign exchange reserves cushion (currently US$300bn).

Despite concerns that record international portfolio flows may at some stage reverse and are putting upward pressure on the Rupee, the government has so far rejected the need to impose capital controls or intervene in the currency markets. More strategically the government is seeking to expand India's low share of global markets (1.3%) by diversifying export markets in Asia through regional Free Trade Agreements (e.g. Singapore, ASEAN, South Korea). The ongoing FTA negotiation with the EU is another key target.

Although the domestic outlook is bright, the downturn reinforced long-standing caution on opening the economy, especially in the financial sector. Many observers hoped liberalisation would proceed more quickly after the Government's re-election in 2009 but there has been little progress, notwithstanding some recent positive hints of movement on the previously off-limits retail sector. India also needs to make itself more attractive to foreign investment (currently 134 out of 183 in the World Bank's Ease of Doing Business rankings).

Looking ahead, in the medium term India expects to sustain high growth but faces key challenges; to maximise its "demographic dividend" (half the population is under 25 years, growing fastest in the poorest states); creating jobs and developing a more labour-intensive manufacturing sector to employ this workforce; generating public and private investments in infrastructure, and improving the delivery of public services, including education and health.

Bribery is illegal. It is an offence for British nationals or someone who is ordinarily resident in the UK, a body incorporated in the UK or a Scottish partnership, to bribe anywhere in the world.

In addition, a commercial organisation carrying on a business in the UK can be liable for the conduct of a person who is neither a UK national or resident in the UK or a body incorporated or formed in the UK. In this case it does not matter whether the acts or omissions which form part of the offence take place in the UK or elsewhere.

Corruption is well entrenched in India and pervades many aspects of daily life. Corruption is often cited as a barrier to the effective development of the private sector and poses business risks that require pro-active management in the form of regular due diligence exercises and up-to-date risk strategies.

Procurement practices often lack transparency and are usually coupled with a significant bureaucratic burden. These risks require careful management.

Politicians, bureaucrats and law enforcement officials often wield significant discretionary power and notable abuses have been brought to light. Several high-profile prosecutions in recent years have helped highlight that the legal framework for fighting corruption exists although enforcement is often weak and responses vary from State to State.

The Indian Prime Minister has targeted corruption as a barrier to India's efforts to 'march ahead as a nation' and the Indian Government regularly blacklists companies known to offer bribes from bidding for defence contracts.

In 2010, India was ranked 87 of 178 countries in Transparency International's Corruption Perceptions Index.

A KPMG survey Bribery and Corruption: Impact on Economy and Business Environment - a series of high-level corruption scandals covered in media over the past two years prompted KPMG Forensic in India to roll out a survey questionnaire to leading corporate to get their insights on the subject of bribery and corruption.

The survey, in January 2011, produced a quick analysis of the responses. The report was released in March 2011 at a press conference, by Dr. Surjit Bhalla, Economist and Chairman Oxus Research and

Investments, Anupama Jha, Executive Director, Transparency International India, Deepankar Sanwalka and Rohit Mahajan.

Visit the Business Anti-Corruption portal page providing advice and guidance about corruption in India and some basic effective procedures you can establish to protect your company from them.

Terrorism Threat

Check out the latest political and economic updates on India.

The Centre for the Protection of National Infrastructure also provides protective security advice to businesses.

The threat posed by numerous domestic and international terrorist groups in India is substantial. Coordinated terrorist attacks in locations frequented by foreigners and expatriates in Mumbai in November 2008 highlighted the increasing risk of collateral damage in India.

Attack locations across major cities in India have included hotels, railway systems, hospitals, markets, cinemas, restaurants, mosques and other open public areas. It is likely that future attacks could target Western iconic locations and those places frequented by foreigners and expatriates.

There are a number of terrorist groups active and operational in India, with a substantial threat posed by

Islamist extremist groups such as Lashkar-e-Tayyiba (LeT) and Jaish-e-Mohammed (JeM) whose aims have spread beyond the secession of Indian-controlled Kashmir to the establishment of a Caliphate in South Asia. Radical left-wing and Maoist groups such as the Naxalites originating in West Bengal also threaten the operation of business in India.

These loosely united groups are engaged in what is described as the Naxalite-Maoist insurgency across numerous states of south, east and south-east India, and involving anywhere up to 20,000 individuals. Attacks have targeted India and Western commercial interests, and have disrupted business operations in affected regions.

Chapter 22: Snapshot of Country Profile

India is among the most popular investment destinations in the world thanks to its low labour costs and stable political climate. India has liberalised the economy during the last 20 years and the government has a business-friendly policy. On the other hand, the business climate is hampered by a cumbersome bureaucracy and pervasive corruption at all levels of government. The political system is characterised by deep-rooted patronage systems and public officials often have vested interests in their positions. Corporate integrity is also very low, as scandals regularly highlight Indian companies' payment of kickbacks both when operating inland and abroad. The federal structure of government means that the level of corruption and the responses to it vary a lot from state to state.

Positive developments in relation to corruption and investment

The Right to Information Act 2005 (RTI Act) has worked as a powerful instrument to enhance governance transparency. The RTI Act grants access to administrative documents within 30 days and has been actively used to hold public officials accountable for their decisions and to monitor public spending.

The Supreme Court has taken some bold steps by upholding corruption charges in cases involving politicians and high-ranking government officials.

The government has striven to simplify administrative procedures and to reduce physical encounters with public officials that could open the way for facilitation payments.

The National Portal of India is a good example of these simplification efforts. In September 2010, in a move to strengthen the country's anti-corruption regulatory framework, a Draft National Anti-Corruption Strategy was unveiled by the Central Vigilance Commission (CVC).

The Indian government is (once again) working on the establishment of a Lokpal (an Ombudsman), after the Lokpal Bill had been introduced to the Parliament eight times in the past decades.

Risks of corruption

Public servants have very wide discretionary powers offering the opportunity to extort undue payments from companies and ordinary citizens.

The numerous bodies charged with combating corruption have conflicting mandates and suffer from a lack of qualified staff and funding.

The awarding of public contracts is notoriously corrupted, especially at the state level. Scandals involving high-level politicians have highlighted the payment of kickbacks in the healthcare, IT and military sectors.

Chapter 23: New Era in UK-India Trade Relations

A new era of business relations between the UK and India is in the best interests of both countries; Justice Secretary Kenneth Clarke told Indian political and business leaders during a visit to promote the UK's legal services industry to one of the UK's biggest potential global partners.

Mr. Clarke spent three days in Delhi highlighting the mutual benefits of increasing the levels of legal business between the two countries. In particular, he gave his full backing to work to liberalise India's legal services.

The Indian legal market is currently estimated to be worth 4 billion dollars, growing to $6.5 bn in 2016 but if fully liberalised its value to India could be $12.3 bn.

Mr. Clarke also meets prominent Indian business people and lawyers to promote the UK as a centre of excellence for litigation and alternative dispute resolution. Mediation and arbitration are quicker, easier and cheaper ways for businesses to solve disputes and it is estimated that mediation alone could save businesses up to £1.4bn a year.

As he arrived in India, Mr Clarke said. "The UK and India are among the oldest and most vibrant democracies in the world. We share an unshakeable commitment to prosperity and freedom which we are trying to realise through economic and political reform. The challenge now is to step up this relationship which is critical to Britain and to the world."

"India is an emerging economic powerhouse and a key player on the international stage. Mr. Clarke also said that "in my meetings with influential Indian business people I did make the case that restrictions on international law firms and foreign lawyers are holding back inward investment and growth in India. Liberalisation is a vital contributor to India's future economic success, while an India that is more receptive to international trade would be hugely beneficial to the UK as an exporter."

The Justice Secretary, who is the UK's International Anti-Corruption Champion, delivered a lecture at the British High Commission in India, in which he discuss the recent implementation of the Bribery Act in the UK and how UK experience in this field could assist India.

Mr Clarke's visit coincides with the first anniversary of the "Enhanced Partnership" announced by Prime Ministers David Cameron and Manmohan Singh in September 2010. Since then trade between India and the UK has grown by 20% to £13 billion, with exports increasing 37%; significant steps towards the Government's ambition of doubling UK-India trade by 2015.

Chapter 24: How to Invest in India

India is officially known as the Republic Of India. It is geographically situated in South Asia, it is the seventh largest country in the world, the second most populated and the largest democracy in the world. It is surrounded by sea on three sides, the Indian Ocean in the south, the Arabian Sea in the west and the Bay of Bengal in the east. Its neighbours are Pakistan in the west, China, Nepal and Bhutan in the north east and Bangladesh and Myanmar in the east. To its south is Sri Lanka. India is the birthplace of Indus Valley Civilization and four important religions Hinduism, Buddhism, Jainism and Sikhism have their roots in India.

Doing business in India after independence was difficult, because India followed a socialistic model of economic growth after independence. The industrial policy was for most part through public sector enterprises and greater emphasis was laid on agricultural sector. Private sector partnership was negligible and the doors for foreign trade were for most part closed. But this model of economic growth failed miserably and by the early 1990's India was faced with serious economic challenges. That is when the government decided to initiate reforms and encourage business ventures by both domestic private industries and foreign companies.

The economic reforms initiated in India after 1991, created an environment conducive for undertaking business in India. The government created a favourable climate for foreign investors to invest in India by relaxing procedures for entry.

India has a bilateral investment treaty with the UK which makes provision for the settlement of disputes between investors of the contracting parties through negotiation, conciliation and arbitration.

India is also a party to the Convention establishing the Multilateral Investment Guarantee Agency (MIGA), which provides for settlement of disputes between State parties to the Convention and MIGA through negotiation, conciliation and arbitration. India has authorised automatic FDI approvals in many sectors.

Foreign investors do not generally need government licenses or approvals and simply notify the Reserve Bank of India of their investments. However, exact rules vary from industry to industry.

A foreign firm could invest in India either by having a wholly owned subsidiary, by having a joint venture with an Indian company or by having a liaison, project and branch office. FDI investment up to 100 per cent is allowed in most sectors with or without permission from government, since India is one of the signatories of WTO. Over a period of time more and more sectors of the economy have been opened up for the foreign investment.

The Reserve Bank of India regulates all foreign exchange transaction and foreign exchange is governed by the Foreign Exchange Management Act 1999. Brands and inventions registered in other countries have been given protection through trademark and patent laws. Usually a trade mark is registered for ten years and a patent is registered for twenty years. By making certain changes to the Patents Act 1970, product patent governance has been brought in.

India has signed Double Taxation Avoidance Agreement (DTAA) with several countries to ensure there is no double taxation. Taxes could be on income from royalty, capital gains, fee for technical services, operational profits accruing from India. To bring about greater accountability and transparency in sales tax and to bring in uniformity in tax charged across the country Value Added Tax (VAT) was introduced from April 1 2005.

The government has allowed for FDI investment in certain sectors through the automatic route, though there could be a cap for the maximum amount of investment. For instance FDI in airports is allowed up to 100 per cent, but any percentage above 74 per cent would require government approval. Again for telecom, FDI allowed is 74 per cent, but for any FDI above 49 per cent government approval is needed. In recent times the government gave permission for some more sectors for FDI .FDI up to 51 per cent was allowed for retail trade, subject to prior permission.

The other sectors which came under the purview of FDI are manufactures of industrial explosives, dangerous chemicals, establishing Greenfield airports and cash and carry wholesale trading and export trading. Investment in certain specified areas like Export Processing Zones, Electronic Hardware technology Park and Software Technology Park are also included in the gamut of automatic route.

Chapter 25: Conclusion

If you are planning moving into the Indian market; don't assume things are the same, no matter how British your business partners may be.

The general rule that nobody follows is that they assume that business is done the same way in their home country. It's the natural reflex.

It gets accentuated in a country like India. If you go to China, you're reminded more obviously that you're in a foreign country. In India, you may be lured into complacency. The differences are still there.

If you expect something to take a week, it'll take a month. There's the timing perception. If the average British businessman wants to do something in one week, it will take four times as long. If you're a person who gets impatient, you shouldn't be the one doing the deal.

You're not that important even if you're the CEO of a FTSE 100 company. Thing is your perception of your self-importance. If you're one of the FTSE 100 companies, your assumption would be you'll be treated in a certain manner, because you're used to being treated in that manner in your home country. That is not a good assumption. The CEO of a major UK company took his private plane to India with his team, and he assumed he didn't even need a visa. But in India you need a visa.

The authorities gave him 24 hours and they fetched him and deported him. That's the way the system works. You can't assume you'll be treated with an amount of deference and respect."

If you're like most British corporations, you'll choose Delhi for your Indian headquarters "Mumbai is like New York and Delhi is like Washington, D.C. A lot more business is done in Delhi. It's also the most livable city.

The government is hiring there. There's better infrastructure; more cleanliness. Lots of British and American corporations are based there. If you have to travel two times a week to talk to the government, you might as well be here."

But expect to travel all over India to do business. You really can't do business by staying in one city; your base is just where your airport is. Visit the Delhi airport at 6 a.m., and it's filled with people who are going to another city. Everything is two hours away.

There's not enough business in any city. You can't just sit in Delhi; you have to go to five cities. You can be a lawyer in London, and never leave London. People travel a lot in India because they need to capture the market.

Expect to start and end your day late. Business in the morning starts late, people have more breakfast meetings. Generally around 10, 10:30.

Dinner time in India also tends to be late. At 6 p.m., people are still having evening tea.

Prepare for things to change at the last minute. Meetings often get scheduled at the last minute, and often change at the last minute. One of the major management consulting firms I represented wanted to schedule a dinner at 6 p.m. in Delhi. I said, 'Nobody will come to your dinner.' People showed up at 9 and 10 p.m. This gentleman didn't listen to me. I told him it's your fault scheduling thinking you have the self-importance to schedule an early dinner.

Even though your Indian counterparts may speak English, there are still language barriers. Most people speak English. That's an advantage you have, but that doesn't mean everything translates. People say, 'no problem' but there can be a number of problems."

Before booking any trip to India, look at all the religious holiday calendars. There are more religious holidays in India. Don't plan a trip right in the middle of them. You could encounter four days of holidays.

Address people by their last names. You don't jump to first names quickly. But that can change people are open to the idea.

Remember not to go in for a handshake with a woman. Generally you would not shake hands with a woman. But no one is getting terribly upset if you do it. That's another thing you need to know.

And you don't need the perfect handshake. In The UK and USA, you have to have a firm handshake. In India, you shouldn't read anything into a limp handshake. A full handshake is not as common. They are more relaxed about that.

Good Luck!

www.ingramcontent.com/pod-product-compliance
Lightning Source LLC
Chambersburg PA
CBHW051716170526
45167CB00002B/685